Heart Whispers

A Mother's Unfiltered Words of Grief

JOANNE MOÏSE-ROUTHIER

Heart Whispers:
A Mother's Unfiltered Words of Grief

Disclaimer
This book contains the ideas and opinions of its author. The intention of this book is to provide information, helpful content, and motivation to readers about the subjects addressed. It is published and sold with the understanding that the author is not engaged to render any type of psychological, medical, legal, or any other kind of personal or professional advice. No warranties or guarantees are expressed or implied by the author's choice to include any of the content in this volume. The author shall not be liable for any physical, psychological, emotional, financial, or commercial damages, including, but not limited to, special, incidental, consequential, or other damages. The reader is responsible for their own choices, actions, and results.

1st Edition. 1st printing 2023

Cover Concept and Interior Design: Stephen Walters, Oxygen Publishing Inc.

Independently Published by
Oxygen Publishing Inc.
Montreal, QC, Canada
www.oxygenpublishing.com

ISBN: 978-1-990093-84-5
Imprint: Independently published

Dedication

To Don,

thank you for believing in me, supporting me,
helping me to find my courage,
and giving me strength when I had none;
and the greatest gift of your Love.

and

To my heavenly son Jesse,
together we forever hold the Flame of Love.

Contents

 Foreword

Juli Lynch, Ph.D

Reading Joanne's raw, emotional, at times gut wrench-ing and heartbreaking story of her journey into grief after the loss of her beloved son brought me to tears. It was through those tears however that I found healing within myself for a lifetime's grief. That is how powerful this story of profound loss and deep darkness is; a search for meaning and eventually a transformation of spirit and soul renewal. This book deeply touched my heart and helped me understand the primordial grief that eventually touches every human. It will do the same for any reader that enters the intimacy of Joanne's personal journey.

Joanne is a gifted energy healer, Reiki practitioner and equine facilitated coach, but her story speaks to the unimaginable and spirit crushing pain of the loss of a child. She reveals her initiation into a healing journey that would tear her heart open, leaving it exposed and then alchemized into a whole new realm of knowing, understanding, and accepting of the Divine and unconditional Love available beyond human experience.

In the years that I've known Joanne she has shown to be a gifted healer, a sister in spirit who knows the alleviating power of horses, recognizes their sacred wisdom and ability to transform the depths of human suffering within the gentleness of their presence. Joanne shared with me the stories of the troubled youth she has guided in her equine facilitated healing programs. I saw her gifts of knowing beyond the physical realm and her ability to bring in the wisdom of spirit. Joanne's initiation into a journey of light through the depths of darkness could not have been foretold, but clearly she was chosen because there was an intention that she would emerge as a Master healer, teacher, and guide.

Joanne takes her readers beyond the telling of the story of her son Jesse's passing, and beyond the story of his struggle with addiction. She takes her readers to a place of intimate details of her day-to-day survival, where her reality and sanity are challenged, her rage is unleashed, her devastation is laid bare, and her questions are unanswered. Why? She asks over and over again. Why? She allows us to see that her strength and connection to spirit withers to but a gossamer thread, fragile and disappearing in the wind. It is raw and beautiful, tragic and poetic.

But she also shares how spirit finds a way back into her heart – her daughter's words on Christmas Eve, a tree that shows her the seasons of grief, her horses that hold her again and again – never wavering in their unconditional Love for her, and finally Jesse's reaching out to her through the veils to show her their new journey together.

Joanne conveys to her readers that grief is like the seasons – ever changing… that grief is the unknowing of day-to-day changes within the seasons – sometimes dark and stormy, sometimes sunshine with a cool breeze. Nature becomes her anchor back to the rhythms of the earth – light and dark, birth and death. Nature becomes her portal back to the Divine.

This is a book for anybody who has ever lost a beloved. This book is for anyone who wonders what it would be like to experience the profoundest of griefs. This book, manifest in Joanne's actual journal entries is so honest, so authentic, so personal, that you will feel her heart inside your own. She doesn't offer a "happy ending," but instead a truthful and transformational conclusion – a resolution that embraces hope, renewal of the alchemic transformation of an initiate into the deepest meanings and knowings of the precious beauty of life.

Juli is Founder of Epala – Equine Partnerships

Introduction

It was hard for me to share these words as a grieving mother. In August 2022, I lost my son, Jesse.

I know from personal experience that journaling has brought such healing through the grace of God and an understanding of who I am, such as I never knew before. A new me was birthed during my grief. The value of this journey has brought me healing and an even deeper spiritual closeness I never previously felt.

Heart Whispers will bring peace and solace to your personal grief experience. It is crucial to be witnessed and heard in the throes of your pain with Love and compassion, and experience a personal flow of grace. I bear sacred space by holding the hands and hearts of every one of you.

I will bring forth emotions. Let it flow! I purposely left pages blank within each chapter to allow the movement of grief through to the other side. This is a transformation of the pain carried within, and expressed in a meaningful way for us and our loved ones to comprehend.

I offer up Heart Whispers to lessen your fear of grief. As a mother I reach out to all the Moms and others grieving the loss of a loved one or anything meaningful and heartfelt. I offer you such profound Love to hopefully achieve even momentarily an easier path, knowing that you too are understood in the wake of the storm.

I wrote in my journal about the first six months after Jesse's passing, and I share my most vulnerable and deepest pieces of myself as I open up to the world. I feel a strong pull that this will help other grieving hearts. This world can use healing guidance; let this be a huge part of the needed healing.

My son Jesse was a great human being. It is tearing me apart to write about him in the past tense. He loved life and loved people. He was the life of the party and had a sense of humour. He had lots of friends, acquaintances, and business relationships.

He started hockey at age four and through commitment and dedication made it all the way to the travelling teams. No matter what Jesse did, he did it with heart, always did his best, and held everyone's best interest. So much so that he often put himself on the back burner, and didn't see that he was important too and that his hurts were just as valid. So he buried his pain and masked it with alcohol, then surfaced into addiction. Addiction falls under the category of an illness of the mind and is very real, and I am bringing this awareness to the world, as there is no shame or reason to hide it. Addiction is a struggle and Jesse was no different; when you hide from it, it just progresses into deeper struggles until you need professional guidance.

At a young age, he knew he wanted to own his own business one day. With perseverance and hands-on experience as a flooring installer, he created Regal Hardwood Flooring and soon after opened a flooring showroom store.

I can praise Jesse until the cows come home. I am a proud Mom of a beautiful soul that left too young. God had a better plan for him, and I know I am part of it as I write this today.

I went down this path to honour Jesse and our unique and special relationship that only we knew the depths of, but everyone around us felt and so respected. This is pure evidence that he, as a spirit, is helping me write this book, and my inspiration came from far deeper than myself.

When Love is this deep between a Mom and Son, the unbreakable bond we shared is still alive today as the Love is still flowing between us, and I will forever honour Jesse in all that I do.

The day I walked out in my back field, I knew I had to set him and myself free to be able to connect fully from the earth side to the spirit side. I had to let him go and set him free; the hardest thing I ever did, so that he could soar to the spirit of his new self.

Through my tears of anguished heartaches, I asked Jesse to show me a sign that he heard me and was with me in releasing our physical heart ties. No sooner had I started my walk back home, I looked straight ahead and there on the cedar tree was a perched BUTTERFLY with solid golden orange flecks, the Eastern Coma. It was facing downwards, enough to say, "Mom, I am here, and I will watch over you." I couldn't believe what my eyes, through streams of tears, were seeing and what my heart felt as I stood there watching, my body trembling.

I knew at that moment our journey together was just the beginning of our HEART WHISPERS.

Part I

Life as I Knew It

AUGUST 9, 2022

Life as I Knew It

"Transmuting the Dusk of Grief to the Rising Dawn of Light and Love!"
– Joanne Moïse-Routhier

On my birthday I sit outside honouring my higher power and myself, setting up for a great day of celebration of me here on Earth. Yes, it is my birthday. Shining my light and gifts to make and create a better place on Earth. I know it happens as my energy surges and evolves to grow within this whole universe. I am part of the whole. Yes, I matter greatly, and so does everyone else. We are all light and Love. We flicker at different frequencies. When we understand who and where we are, we automatically evolve and bring others with us. This is how intelligent the universe is. We will share this awareness as we jump into the Waters of Love and light. They coexist with the powers of protection and balance, and bask in the purities and facts that they are. We start with small dips, and our thirst for more is recurrent dips and then deeper dips, until we fully submerge as we understand what is contained therein. We swim in delight as the sun hits the surface waters in twinkling lights, supporting our destiny to the island.

This island destination is where our eyes adjust to the overwhelmingness of finally arriving at the clarity we have been searching for. The delight it holds is the healing and freeing of our Souls that we never thought imaginable. We did the inner work. Higher Divine guidance, where we were divinely magnetically drawn to. Our inner guidance, housed within our Soul and contains Spirit, has brought us to where we are to be, and where our gifts are revealed. We only wish and desire to feel what we know is capable of being housed for each and every one of us. Let the beauties unveil as we ascend with the Divine, and our natural gifts shine to and for all.

AUGUST 11, 2022

Welcome to this Sacred Land

It is a vortex of magic and invitation. It is healing. I sit here as the sun rises into the early time of the coming day. I set my intention to own this magic I carry, of the power that I witness from the Divine. I sit in delight with my God, as I bask in the potential of creation with Love and light.

I am beyond amazed at this human container that houses this amazing element of energy I am.

This world is the kingdom that holds all I am. I am already speechless, but I know I am a channel for the DIVINE, to do greater things than I could have imagined. MY ANGEL AND GUIDES ARE WITH ME ALWAYS. I have to be open and conscious of their presence and allow their messages to be received. Today, I surrender and allow God's work through me, as I have prepared by doing my routine clearing of yesterday's remanence. I am open to today's gifts.

AUGUST 12-14, 2022

Mother's Intuition

I had a strong sense of yearning for my son Jesse, and I sent him these words on Saturday…

"It really would have been nice to have you here today, Jesse. All the excitement of doing hay and having a BBQ; just spending some time here. I really wish you would have come here, maybe after Eric's house. I know you are busy and all, but I don't know, Jess, it would really be nice to have you here. I miss you. Even if it's just some quiet time. Just getting reacquainted with your country roots."

That evening I sent him a photo of my bonfire, just as he had the night before of the one he was sitting at.

AUGUST 13, 2022

Swirling Thoughts

I sit here and read a lot of stuff and know a lot, so I want to teach this stuff to people, but I don't do anything about it. Why? Is it because I compare myself to my successors? Do I not feel good enough or smart enough? As I write, I have a trigger surface about not being smart in school. Let me tell you, I may not have initials after my name like a Ph.D., but I have so much more in the truth of life as an energetic being and tapping into the mastery of all. Yes, I have that. I have the greatest gifts a human could ask for, but most of all I have the truth of Life Mastery behind my name. This is the root of living its majestic side of life. Heal energetic past blocks in the human energy Power Systems of functionality from the roots. Infuse Love and light, and you will be living your best life with manifestations of desire of the infinite source, available to us all. It's all energy and we are part of the whole. Don't be afraid to pass along success and manifestations to show what it's like feeling it versus doing it. When you succeed at a project or anything, it's because your true authentic self was present, and it is the Divine power. The point I am getting at here is when we listen and feel and practice, we develop our gifts that we all hold; the more we practice anything - the better it gets, the stronger it gets, the deeper connection we acquire. This is the way of life first by understanding who you really are, and then where to go from there. Trust me!

These were the final words I had written three days before what happened in the next chapter…

On Sunday, August 14th, the worry and fear set in, and I started reaching out to Jesse's friends who would have seen him last, and when they had last heard from him.

AUGUST 15, 2022

The Call

Monday 15th, the real pitted excruciating gut experience of knowing and putting steps in motion, calls to close friends and then the final call to the police to do a wellness check…

5:19 P.M. THE CALL that brought me to my knees in a scream the far end of the world could have heard….

HE'S GONE

Part 2

The Internal Storm – WHY's

Raw Real Grief

*"Life changed me. I would never be the same,
faith that is all I am/was left with." – Joanne Moïse-Routhier*

I BEG AND PLEAD

The day my life changed with the traumatizing news after the three days of my "mother's intuition," heightened to a point where I knew something was wrong. The call came in to tell me my son was gone. He had passed away. He was found the day after he passed.

Dear God, Jesus Lord Angel guide me… How am I even writing this…? How do I put words down…? How am I going to do this…? Why God, why…?

I start this part of the journey with the Lord's prayer. I prayed to the Father, Son and Holy Spirit; the three parts of the great One. I take a piece of it and light it up within myself. I pray for personal miracles and evolutions and transformation in my growth forward; for the fog to lift. Here's a piece about my healing that brings in light at a distance. I pray for this unknown road to be paved with blessed rocks as I step onto each one. I sit with each meaning until the next one appears. I pray for clarity in direction and to cleanse my pain with Love. I pray to deepen my Love and to live life to my guided capacity. I pray for my connection to deepen with the Spirit world and acquire the messages I am meant to receive. I pray for the greatest co-creativeness I have ever had, to build the unknown service work and the ability of doing greatness with people into the likes of which I have never imagined. I pray to co-create the gift of Jesse's spirit to work with me to fruition here on Earth, i.e. my personal journaling and holding his meaningful coin, the one Jesse wanted me to have, and to know what I needed to do to reach for the stars. I pray for it to serve all that is needed. I pray to somehow work with people from areas of addiction. I pray to put my personal Love of life into this work. I pray my journaling inspires people who need it. I pray to bring the work I do with my horses in a therapeutic fashion, to co-create a change in the world for all who need this self-transformation to desired outcomes to ease their grief. But mostly, I pray for my healing journey. I pray for continued Angels to show up like they have, and I pray for inspiration, courage and health by the grace of God.

SEPTEMBER 14, 2022 - ONE MONTH

The Portal Exit

I'm angry, upset and confused. "WHY did you have to leave, why?" I still don't fully comprehend that he is in the spirit world, and I'm just kidding myself by remaining in disbelief of this fact. Why is this happening/ed?

I am hyper breathing writing this, and I cannot believe I am doing this little, going through this. As I piece together the days up to THE CALL, I have questions. I never shared what transpired the last time I was with Jesse. I didn't put it together until I spoke with my mentor Dr. Juli Lynch. I never shared this with anyone, of what I knew to question. I knew the right time would come, and who would help me reveal this knowing, as what happened was deep. This went on for four months. What happened physically to me, I knew, was just plain darkness, but what was it? I knew Juli would be able to discern what happened about my physical sickness and heart pain. It was like I was going to have to go to the emergency as a heart attack was coming on.

It was explained so clearly; some may not know about any of this, but remember I am very spiritual. I am awake and know there is a force greater than ourselves, and it happened to me and through me.

Jesse chose me. I was the PORTAL he entered as Spirit, the TRANSITIONAL period. His body needed to leave (die) as his Spirit had already left the night I was there with him back in June, through me… wow! The portal of his exit.

In the Bible it states clearly that 40 days and 40 nights is how long it took for Jesus to leave his body; Jesse was 50.

Juli explained that people with greater gifts and have things to do from the other side, for the humans on Earth usually leave between the ages of 32-35. Jesus was 32. Jesse was 35.

She also told me to look up the story of Jesus and Mary, the bond of Mother and Son.

I also shared that deep down I knew I didn't want to return until Jesse was underway in clearing up his life, as I felt his DARKNESS was so heavy that I couldn't go back.

My Soul knew I couldn't go back, that's why there was resistance because Jesse had entered the portal; it wasn't my time to go, for he was in it and there was nothing I could do.

I know this is unbelievable, and not just anyone will be able to follow what I am sharing. But I am for those that will be making sense of this and bring awareness to others.

It has been determined through my conversation with Juli how psychic I am for all that occurred in the past four months. I needed to have these pieces put together, and I am beyond blessed to have Juli in my life to make sense of what I thought I knew and to question what it all meant. I kept quiet for these months until the truth of what transpired came.

SEPTEMBER 20, 2022

Dear God

I beg you to help me with this pain of grieving for my son. I cannot fathom ever being ok again. Help me, please.

My heart is in physical pain and my body is shaking. Tears are rolling down and my throat is tight and constricted in pain and sorrow. I cannot believe I will never see Jesse on Earth again. I'm gasping for air. How am I going to go through this? He was my everything, my go-to; he was my life. As time and life are moving on and settling around me, the grief within my heart is growing deeper and deeper with pain. How will life ever be the same? Angels, I beg you all to surround and hold me as I cannot get up from the ground. The pain from this grieving is getting worse, and I'm scared of how I'm feeling in such despair. My whole body is constricting… tears… sorrow… have consumed me…

I DON'T KNOW WHAT TO DO.

Joanne Moïse-Routhier

The Leaves

As I sit and look outside, I see the apple tree in a new way. It's a vision of my feelings within my heart. The leaves are falling as the fall starts to set in; a sign of Mother Nature at this time of year. The leaves for me represent fragments of my heart breaking apart and falling to the ground. The pain in my heart has slowly turned to numbness and has nothing left to hold on to as a whole. The pain is too unbearable to hold on to and so it falls on its own. I am left to feel empty as the tree will be. I only pray that Mother Nature in her holding of the dried-up leaves on the ground, can nurture that process of the greatness it possesses. For me I see the leaves falling and the tree getting emptier and emptier, just like my heart and Soul.

SEPTEMBER 25, 2022

Unresolved Wound

I noticed how I want to stay in my grief. It keeps me close to Jesse and also it keeps me at the attention of others. I asked myself why? Why am I hungry for others to want me? Was I so lonely as a child? Was I emotionally abandoned? Physically abandoned? OMG YES! This is possibly the biggest VOID of emptiness I carry. Is this why the food I eat is crap and that I overeat, and then shame myself about it? VICIOUS CYCLE. It's not about telling me to just STOP, it's about asking why and what is going on. The root has surfaced and now I am healing it! I need to be witnessed in my grief.

I just sat in the pain of that little girl's abandonment emotions (heart and throat constrictions,) and held her and talked to her and took her with the adult me filled with Love, and healed her broken heart and merged her into the NOW ME adult version. The memory of the place of abandonment is still there but the little girl is not. She has been rescued, recovered, found the SELF and now resides in a healed heart. I re-envisioned the past picture memory of who I was and the age I was then, so when I think back, she is no longer there; the pain has been recovered and merged in healing into the here and now with Love. That past trauma has been healed. I can now let that go (big sigh,) and move on with such less heaviness and the shedding of layers of much-needed healing.

Today Love has grown in my heart!

OCTOBER 2, 2022

Lost Soul

Sitting in my chair I feel the increased tightness in my stomach, eyes swelling… here it comes again. As I reflect on last evening, sitting outside on the barrel in the horse arena watching the sun set. My heart breaking over again I asked what happened GOD? Why did you have to go Jesse? He was a lost Soul in great pain, this I know and I know he knew that I knew too. The desire to be helped was not bigger than his pain. To me, he wanted to numb it down more than seek the help available. I'm twisted and constricted in heartache and I still can't believe he is gone. I pray to God and the Angels for me to have a productive day as I now watch the sun rise. I ask it to shine on my heart for today. I don't want to stay in this state of remembrance of his pain. I want to remember his greatness in all areas of his life. I was so proud to be his Mom. He was the life of the party everywhere he went. He made everyone feel special. His heart was bigger than the galaxy.

OCTOBER 9, 2022

Better Plan

I know God has a better plan, always does, than we humans think. Your time here Jesse was on purpose, and your Soul succeeded in what it came to do. I see that clearly as everyone that you came across, you touched them in a very special way. You left a powerful imprint on each and everyone's heart. God knew he could call upon you and do greater work from a special place, with even more intense Love than you or anyone could imagine. I am blessed and honoured, Jesse, you chose me to be your Mom. Not only did you come into this world through me, but you also chose to leave this world through me. This is not an everyday experience for just anyone. Jesse, with all our chats about God and the greater picture, you knew you could safely and in a comforting place to exit, chose our Love to transition you to the higher plane and on to your next journey. I do ask you, son, to show me a sign of your new home and the work together we are to do. But you did send me a sign, many as a matter of fact.

A Little More Each Day

I pray to open my self up a little more each day, for my greatest good of all; to receive more and to see and feel more, to open up all the senses to their highest level.

I take time today now to sit quietly, to be with God and all Angels to guide me into where I am to be.

I trust and have faith more and more to show up for me in my directional path with ease and Love.

Trauma and Shock

I notice right away I'm pissed at everything… I hate it all! I just want to scream for fuck sake (tears rolling,) why, why, why GOD? What lesson is it for me and who would want this "losing a son" experience? The traumatic experience? Watching the wheel start rolling in slow motion (a movie reel,) of what's to come of the excruciating pain of getting the news "your son is gone…" and the world went blank and black.

I now put pieces of what transpired in my body and psyche the following day. I remember getting up and all I wanted for my trembling body, which barely sustained its weight to carry my walking steps, was to have a warm bath. I couldn't be any shakier nor more frozen in body temperature. The buildup of the whole weekend tragedy and how I was feeling, and all the signs and emotions coming into the moment of the news, and the hurried rush drive to the destination right up to the next day; I was in an altered state and my body went into traumatic shock.

I am writing all that comes to me and make note of the importance of following and trusting our inner gut. Your body is speaking a truth language to be followed. I learned/ing to listen more and more and it speaks loud and clear. Same as your GUT INTUITION (Soul/Spirit,) it knows. Tap into it and trust it, it's never ever wrong. Trust me, I know.

OCTOBER 14, 2022

The Fragmented Mess

I look around the house and I see each room is a total mess. Things not put away, clutter, not clean, accumulated stuff all over. I just realized looking out is the same reflection of my inner ping-pong of the emotional state my world is… I AM A MESS.

This is about the state of me and the mess I'm in. I'm grasping at, again too many things to sort, and all it's doing is showing up literally worse and worse within my surroundings.

I just want to cry… I am… Lost… So lost… tears and my heart is shattered.

OCTOBER 25, 2022

Gut Kick

I had an eye-opening gut-wrenching awakening of my grief. It's scary territory I'm embarking on, vulnerable at its core. Unknown roadway and unchartered waters and diving deep is making me weak. (Joseph Campbell's *Hero's Journey*.)

As I travel on this road I will never be the same, I am changed forever and how? I don't know. I am only taking the "courage steps" to move forward and see what transforms, as I know this is truth.

The worst thing to happen in your grief is being shut down in your attempt to be witnessed during a vulnerable moment. That was like being kicked in the gut and never seeing it coming, and knocking the wind right out of me in mid-breath. Yap!

It happened, not maliciously, just out of their own self-preservation to not get personally caught up in their own grief, their fear of grief.

OCTOBER 27, 2022

The Trees

As I stand watching the trees bare their leaves, I am witnessing the seasons change. I am drawn inwards like I am part of the tree, due to the fact I too am changing and baring my Soul. The old me is losing "itself," and I feel RAW and BARE, the equivalence of VULNERABLE to what is happening inside of me. I will be just like the tree that is bare over the winter, resting and preparing for the next season.

For now, it's withdrawn into itself. I will emerge from my new self. I am in hibernation, the rawest form of transitioning in this journey of grieving. I will be gentle with myself as I observe, absorb, heal and regenerate in strength and knowingness I never knew. Because I will be renewed, I will and am going through a rebirth.

I feel I'm crawling into the cocoon stage of self-protection and preservation while I gain awareness and emerge into what is, for now, the unknown.

NOVEMBER 2, 2022

I Am The Fog

As I wake I immediately felt the pain in my heart center and the sensation of overwhelmedness to be hugged and held; a needed hug sensation with tremendous tears and sobs. I had to sit with a pillow on my core center and rock and squeeze it. I envisioned Jesse's arms around me and holding me tight.

As I look in the distant fields ahead sitting in my living room journaling, I see the FOG. I feel a sense of it like watching a movie where you see at a distance the rolling fog. The faint appearance of a loved one from the spirit world. I had to get up and go outside and be with the fog. Holding that feeling I walked in it and took photos and in my streaming tears I said, "I know you're there but I can't see you."

My journey is a connection to where I am, "in the fog of things." I'm trying to find my way through life again, and sometimes the fog is so thick I can't see my next step, so I just stop. I notice my thoughts and emotions. I surrender and allow what is present within me to EMERGE, the energies of "E-motions" (energy in motion) to flow. This release has given me some momentum to carry on to the next step forward. As I look up again, the fog has lifted its thickness just enough for me to see my first few steps ahead.

The sun has dawned just enough to see the silhouette of the tree tops at a distance over the fog, and I feel like I can regulate my breath to my steps forward.

Today's journey has yet to be known and unveiled, just like the fog!

Resilience

Is accepting your new reality right, even if it's less good than the one you had before?

You can fight it, you can do nothing about it BUT scream about the loss, or you can start to accept that it happened and try to put together something that is meaningful and life-changing.

Oh, the pain is horrible in my heart and chest. One day it will settle down into peacefulness.

NOVEMBER 11, 2022

The Spiral

Oh, the pain of life's struggles when we don't know where to turn, and feel alone. It must feel scary, an ever whirlwind. I just want the pain to stop. We do whatever it takes to make it go away quickly as the latter takes too long even for a short while. I get stuck in the polarity of the downward spiral. I don't have the strength to fight it; little own the know-how or the will to. I keep spiralling but think, "I'm good I got this" as the temporary relief of "choice" numbs the pain.

I pray to be the vessel to help guide lost souls to find strength and know there is a way from pain to peace, one swirl at a time, upward. Up is harder, but once the veil has been penetrated, the light starts to shine through the smallest point of entry. The breath starts to slow down, and the glimpse of exiled hope has seeped into the heart of the soul. Now the thread's "twist of turn" redirected to the upward momentum as the heaviness starts to break and fall away, to build a space for the new me to emerge from the chrysalis that held me until I was ready. I know the saving grace call of my saving is from the GOD known to all of us here on Earth. Don't give up, lift up your arms and your hand will be grabbed and held, then guided. You are not alone.

The Meltdown

My first trip to the cemetery. Prior to arriving, I asked for a sign, as I just listened to the song *Signs of a Dove*. I cried to Jesse to show me a sign, maybe a white bird. I was fixated on white, and low and behold, coming out of church on my way to the cemetery it started to snow. How much more of a message was there for me?

Once I returned home, the shock of the outing paralyzed me in numbness of the meltdown that held me captive for the rest of the day. I had a real anger surface for the first time as I hit the pillow over and over. I cried the repeating words, "Why did you have to die, WHY?" The rumbling of anger finally came out in screams so loud my throat went raw and I had no voice.

I have to grieve in my way and time, no one else's. This is me, my journey, the only way to heal is to feel it through, and I am and I will. But oh, the heartache pain is very real.

NOVEMBER 22, 2022

Love, Compassion and Hard Truths

The son I got to know through my grief. What I didn't know was how much pain he masked in his daily living. To this day I never knew how much, why and what was troubling him. I run this over and over in my head, "Why did he have to die?" He didn't mean to nor did he know he was going to transition that early morning when he closed his eyes to just go to sleep. He never woke up here on earth again; he woke up to the heavens.

Addiction is real but not the root of cause.. How did I allow this to go on? I handed him the keys to self-destruction is what I feel as a Mom. I didn't have the tools or knowingness. It was more than just "addiction" or "having fun" in life. There were deep-rooted unexplained inquiries of mental health, and when you don't have the tools to move forward, it just spirals down. It is a dark hole to climb out from. My words to anyone reading; do research on addiction and mental health because addiction is a disease of the mind. I've since studied with Dr. Gabor Maté on Compassionate Inquiry; getting to the root of the problem without judgment, just plain Love and compassion. What I didn't know is hard to claim to know when it's too late. As a Mom, I didn't see through all the facades and red flags, or is it that I didn't want to?

Why Did You Pick Me?

There is nothing that will ever hurt me again, as I am travelling through the most excruciating pain a person can be brought into. There is nothing left inside to hurt. I will never be the same as the previous me. I never knew this eternal Love pain. It only showed up from losing the most cherished part of me… MY SON.

IN THE DEEPEST AND DARKEST PIT I COULD FIND MYSELF AS I WAS STARTING TO BREATHE AGAIN, my only words were, "God please help me" in the drowning of my tears.

This is the only upside I could look to as a 'Hope in Hell' that there is someone listening and make me wake up from this nightmare.

Being brought to my knees from weakness and in the midst of cries for help was the INVISIBLE that my Soul knew and held the power to help and show up in the way it was needed, even for just a second at a time to be released from the intensity of grief's clutches.

The threads of this vice around me were threading downwards, and I (knew) hoped one day those threads were gonna turn the opposite direction and spiral upwards. This is where assistance came in from the

Universal power; my God came in.

I am pleading and begging to be held and guided into the greater picture of my so-called life.

Just this morning, in pure fear and tears I asked, "Why Soul did you pick me and my life to experience such pain, for a mother to witness the heartache trauma of losing her son from the departure of this earth, why?"

Gotta Be More

There's gotta be more to this… surely I just am not given this experience of being crushed and found on the floor after being slammed into a brick wall…?

No, there is more, and this is bringing me to wonder what is more about this?

The beginning of a question period about the whys, what, who, where and when?

I feel an early grief awareness of evolution, as Jesse knew from our relationship that I would get the meaning of the signs; and who to go through to get a message to me.

This is beyond and nothing shy of a transcendence of an awakening to be taught to all.

No word of a lie, as I'm writing this I receive a text from my daughter, Chantale, and this brought me to uncontrollable tears… I cannot believe what I'm about to share as I know this couldn't happen without knowing it's Jesse as the messenger at work… Addiction is real and will take a life if there is no desire… but he knew there was desire with his sister and he stepped in.

Her words; "I AM HAVING TEARS OF JOY. I FEEL LIKE MY BROTHER SAVED MY LIFE… I HAVE BEEN GIVEN A CHANCE TO LIVE LIFE TO THE FULLEST."

DECEMBER 12, 2022

Rock Bottom

My journaling is all I have left to help me go through this. God help me, please I'm feeling so lost right now; from my knees to begging for strength and the pain to show me some direction.

Conversation with Jesse...

"Jesus Jesse, why did you have to go so soon or at all, for that matter.

You help Mom, especially NOW because I can't do it alone or without you. Call on your team because Mom needs an army of helpers right now… Help me, Jesus and Jesse; you are the ones I turn to every day… DAMMIT, YOU LEFT ME… when I was so scared for you and your pain. I hit rock bottom, son, I really did. Now how do I do it? This fkn hurts, and I'm scared shitless in the CLIMB… this rope had better be big and strong to pull me up tug by tug. I'm dead weight, and I don't know if I have the strength or will to be pulled up.

I'm like a struggling horse caught in the muck and needing help but sinking further and further.

Your team will softly pull me little by little with your soft whispers Jesse, to guide me. (Keep going, Mom… listen to music, Mom). I never showed you much of my weakness, but now you get it all, and I need your help. Who would have thought you would be someplace else and begged for help in getting me through the worst a

Mother can possibly go through?"

Now I'm gonna go listen to the song *WHERE I FIND GOD* - by Larry Fleet and Morgan Wallen.

December 16, 2022

Internal Storm

OMG, I was the "internal walking storm" yesterday. Each step was unpredictable in the level of swelling pain upwards to the heart and out in tears. Dear God, that was literal physical pain I never felt before. I literally walked with a live storm going on inside of me. I thank God and Jesse for working miracles that I wasn't alone, as it was his birth date and I met up with Chantale at the cemetery to just be and to talk. I watched from a distance as she sat on the lightly powdered snow-covered ground, talking to her brother. I know she was giving him a huge thank you Love talk, while questioning why it had to be this way. I say thank you to the powers that are at work.

Today I watched the storm happening in a real-life snowstorm. Today is a reflection of what my insides looked like yesterday; the whiteouts that represent much that were not able to be seen, only felt. Parallel to the two storms, I couldn't see my storm, but I certainly could feel it, and the outer storm, I certainly could see it. I thanked it for giving me a break from the inner side of a storm. I am safe inside while the storm outside is happening. I bring myself to flow with it and allow the residue to emerge, as it holds awareness pieces for my healing.

Christmas Eve Gift

In tears, I sat in the Storm on the eve of Christmas in a heartache and was mad at God, "Why couldn't you save my Jesse?" Why did he have to go? I know he was hurting deeply about many things in life, but he was still worthy of saving. I don't get it; I am hurting badly.

I'm thankful for all that my daughter Chantale is doing, and I know Jesse is helping his sister.

I pray for me and my family to go through this tragedy of losing Jesse, and to find a message meaning in each dip into the deep throes of grief and sorrow.

Many are celebrating, but not me this time, for I am lost in deep grief and pain of not having my world with me by my side.

This is my gift from my daughter Chantale, these words:

"Mom, you have to believe that GOD is holding Jesse in his loving arms. His job on earth was completed. And you can be thanked for putting such a beautiful human being in this world. It's very sad, but he was only lent to us by GOD. Now may Jesse rest comfortably knowing that he touched all of our souls deeply and with Love."

I could not have asked for a more beautiful Christmas gift with these words.

DECEMBER 27, 2022

Regrets

I feel as soon as my emotions take healing time, where I'm too drained to think or feel, there's just enough energy to go right back into the throws of grief. Oh, my heart is aching and tears are flowing, and the disbelief of Jesse being gone is unfathomable all over again. I'm sad beyond sad; there are no words, just emotions that are left in the throws of the invisible.

REGRETS are flowing in the mix and bringing in the WHY's… I know I will go through this cycle quite a few times and maybe forever. The key is it will be random forever, not constant forever. No one could survive any measures of the "constant forever" of emotions. The psyche nor the body mechanics would accept this; it automatically goes in the PROTECTIVE/SURVIVAL mode. I am a human (born to survive,) not a machine without needs beyond my thinking abilities in the moment(s). Us as humans carry a body that is a walking and waking miracle. Yes, it needs temporary assistance at times. It's always functioning to return to its natural state so feed it natural medicines.

Safe Cocoon

Life is moving on for the world, and I don't want it to. I am in my cocoon, and this is where I want to stay. Tightly wrapped and with nothing to see, but at the same time so much is transforming within me naturally.

I allow it to take place; truthfully, there is no other choice to go with it. I must "trust the process" to be in a position to fly with new wings when the time comes to emerge like a butterfly with such a magnitude of beauty. To witness the transformation of my Soul's evolution with God's hand in play, I know it will be extraordinary as an unknown that will be first known, like a new birth...

I pray for strength in the meantime and Angel guidance along the way. I feel such a hole in my heart, I pray to heal and hold my heart in the support it needs right now.

JANUARY 17, 2023

Anger & Resentment

I'm gonna share an emotion of resentment as I sit with its attention calling to me, and feeling a rise of intensity toward anger. I got curious to understand its meaning and message to release its clutches, as I do not want any part of someone else's issues. I will say it's a reflection of who they are. What they have and hold within themselves, (a huge sigh of relief from this process). I asked the question: why do I feel it? Is it mine or theirs? Both, so I looked where I held mine as I offered out an olive branch but it wasn't accepted, so I was filled up with hurt, sadness, then upset (my Jesse would never do this or cause such pain to anyone…) and I cried. All of a sudden, I receive a text from my Grandson Ethan showing me a picture of the beautiful morning sunrise. What Divine timing, and I know Jesse had his hands in this and sent an Angel to help me in my demise. You cannot make this stuff up. I now sit with Love and let go of the anger and resentment that holds no space in my heart. Resentment deteriorates the Soul; Love builds it and strengthens our overall. Let this be a reminder of what's important and holds the value and worth of the self. For me, this was a miraculous shift to rejoice in it fully. I bask in this revelation for my whole being to transform this awakening.

JANUARY 26, 2023

Never The Same

It's so hard to get out into the big bad world, I call it. That world is different when you're trying to show up, and the body remembers how it used to be, but now the heart is much different and delicate. The adjustment in meshing these two is not easy, BUT scary. My safe place is my home, my cocoon where I AM DEVELOPING MY NEW WINGS. Life always moves forward during grief; but you don't move with it. It's too fast, too busy, too much. I am in my own world, and I must make it safe. I know I wouldn't be as strong as I am if not for the deep dives into my grief like I did and continue to do so. It's beyond painful at the risk of facing my new reality and my new world. I will not ever wish to be nor go back in time to return to the person I used to be. I will never be the same. I am not the same. I know I am facing a wave of unknown dips of intensities and also calmness. I know I will trust this process for the greatest healing. In my healing journey, a piece of me sometimes evolves with new awareness. I walk on (horse talk) into my journey and dance with the flow of life. I enter my new arena of life and welcome my four partners, Oreo, Belle, Ellie and Max, for my personal therapy healing to continue the miraculous experiences to come forth, as I know it is meant to heal. The "horse power" they provide is not only physical, it's transcendent from humanity for our therapeutic wellness. I have grown and healed pieces I didn't even know existed. I am a better version of myself because of it, which I know to be true.

FEBRUARY 5, 2023

I'm Afraid

I've never been so scared of how I'm feeling since last evening. Depression is what comes to mind as I only cry. My heart aches and I cannot see past the pain. I am so afraid of letting my grip go of holding on to what was of Jesse after he passed.

I am hanging on to threads, such as I wish I could go back to the day of the funeral, even the wake, so that I can spend more time with him there and all the other times before.

This is wreaking havoc on me emotionally. I look tired, run-down, and old. I'm a mess, and I'm afraid.

Finding Myself in Trouble

I'M in emotional, mental and physical trouble. As I look in the mirror, I see burned out, exhausted, and sad heavy eyes looking back, and the words came, "I don't even know who I am at this point."

I must focus and heal myself first. I'm a mess and I gotta get myself turned around or else I will find myself in trouble.

My heart is speaking loud and clear. I need to take action in my mission and passion in life.

I am suffering deep down, and by not doing what I'm here to do, I am creating my own death, and I will physically deteriorate.

FEBRUARY 7, 2023

Grief's Ball and Chain

Today I bared down asking, please God help me and guide me for my fear of not choosing to change. I was heading for the complete ultimate deterioration of myself little by little. A Tarot reader asked me, "What would Jesse say about the state you are in?" I had to rise above and choose to live again. I was slowly tumbling downwards to the means of self-destruction, from the inner pain and fear of living away and onwards from the depths of grief. It was swallowing me inside out. I didn't want to close my eyes to sleep, even for the trauma held in my body that kept me a victim to death. It was taking me down so far I didn't recognize who was in the mirror. I was fading into grief's ball and chain and couldn't find the key to unlocking the bond from my vision, constantly flared and flooded with burning tears. It was due to the mirror reflecting what I feared the most; the "grips of grief" had its hold on me, and it scared me to no end. I know precisely Jesse's words to me. "Mom, get it together and go hold those coins that found their way back to you, from the signs you picked up on that I sent you. I knew the day would come when you would desperately need them Mom, as it clearly says to reach for the stars." The message for me to live again was clearly received, Amen!

FEBRUARY 14, 2023

Day of Hell

I am sad; I am mad on this day called Valentine's.

I want to throw and break things.

I need something to help me today, now! God, I am here; I beg you to cup me in your hands and hold me tightly on this ride of Hell called grief.

I so miss my son.

Part 3

The Emergence

The Emergence

"FAITH - Faith is being sure of what we hope for and certain of what we do not see." — Hebrews 11: 1.

CONNECTION

The stillness of the aftermath; I look around in a state of wonder. I wonder how I survived and came out on the other side. The excruciating pain, this truly physically hurts. I sit in this welcoming stillness where I absorb a moment of "ok-ness" to write at this point.

GOD, I pray for continued guidance on my life's journey and honour my Soul's evolution in its need to be freed, in order to attain what it came to learn and evolve. Who AM I to stop it? I'd be cheating myself if I did.

I acknowledge this and I drink it all in. I thank you, Jesse, for your continued connection and messages throughout the thick and thin of this path called, 'Grieving Your Love and Presence.' We guide each other on this new journey that I am totally naked and raw to. I know I cannot stay in this quicksand, nor would you want me to, nor would this honour you or our Mother / Son relationship we built over 35 years.

In the stillness of meditation after such rolling tears I immediately start to write, and the answers that start flooding through are nothing shy of Soul awakening. A touch of my heart flows through from my inner guidance; my soul is the equivalent of what happens each and every time I put pen to paper.

I learn the practice to listen to my consciousness as it develops my senses and connection to the power we all hold of the almighty Divine within. We connect to the infinite and just trust it. It may not make sense but the pieces of seeds are placed exactly where they fit. Journaling is nurturing to what we sow and we will harvest the best of ourselves along our journey.

Trust the Process

Thank you my friend Lisa.

The sun is rising and shining on the tops of snow-covered trees at a distance reflecting a hue of fog lifting, and calmness and clarity are what I saw and felt. I reflected on the four seasons and they each have their purpose and the cycle never ends. I can begin to see we continuously EMERGE into our new SELF each go around. Trust in the process, it is not only words. It is fact and it is science, and it is amazingly beautiful. Each cycle may have a short or long period of transformation; allow it to happen at its own timing and don't fight it. Trust it and you will be in awe of its messages of growth; it is evolutionary. Remember this is personal, yours and only yours.

Today is a new day and I don't know what it holds. All I know is I surrender and welcome the greatness it brings for my healing, planting of seeds, answers, and curiosity of what each fitting piece holds as a message to my wholesome puzzle.

I feel I'm in a time to deeply heal with a sincere commitment of communion with myself and my GOD and my higher self. Words that are coming to mind… Quiet—Reflect—Birth—Preparation—Unknown   level of connection with mySELF—Shut off— Recluse.

God, what is my greater calling and purpose in my next part of this journey?

OCTOBER 16, 2022

Son-Day

I just said to myself, "Today is Sunday, the weekday Jesse transitioned." It hit me, SON-DAY; it's Jesse's day as well as God's day. There's a reason why God called him on his day and I always honoured Sundays. But now I have had an awakening in how I will have a whole new different perspective of this day when Jesse was called Home to the Lord's Kingdom.

I don't want to be devastated and saddened with tears and pain to relive the day he passed… No.

I thank you guides and Angels for this message in a step of strength on this day.

Dancing With Life

I feel like I am emerging into something that is unknown to me. I feel curiously optimistic about what this will look like. I can say it has lit a flicker of a spark to the dying embers that are left at the bottom of my being.

Could this be it? Words reach the power held in the energy of the feel and meaning behind the sound. Sound has frequency, frequency holds vibration; vibration holds the emotion of where you are consciously and/or subconsciously. Your dominant thoughts create your present situation. It's all in a FEEL. Just like being with the horses, it's a feel for when you're with them; can you feel it with every aspect of being present? The horses would absolutely let you know if you are in communion. Then you will have a check-in with yourself and know exactly where you are at. That is how horses communicate, non-verbally powerful. You will feel the steps together like a dance. You will feel the heart connection between the two of you and there is nothing more beautiful nor gratifying. My search is over.

NOVEMBER 8, 2022

The Impact (OMG)

Thank you Jesse for being and coming here on earth to be my son. My heart is breaking with tears and weeping over our short time together. Please forgive me for any wrong and pain I have brought.

I had time to sit in the presence of my horses, and this came to me:

"I have to say goodbye now as you are going to a new home. God, I miss you. We will always hold in our hearts our Love that was so deep, that anyone around could feel. We radiated our relationship with everyone. I so cherished our time together and I know we connect deeper now on a different level. I know you truly feel our Love as a son and mother even deeper now from where you are… HOME."

I realize now the impact a son has on a mother, me, for me and with me, until they are gone. You feel their impact on how they made you feel; you hear their echoing words that resonate how they made a change for you in so so many unique and individualized and personalized ways. I will forever carry all of them with you in my Heart and Soul. I will always carry you Jesse wherever I am, you/we are forever together. This I know from the pit of my own Soul. I Love you, son.

NOVEMBER 28, 2022

Soul Questions

The pieces are all part of the BIG PICTURE of the puzzle we are birthed with. My Soul knows what it came here to experience in the emotions of events.

But does it know all events us humans can get in the way? How does this happen, is my question. How do events happen in the way the Soul needs the emotions from out of the experience? Is it my life's events or do I learn to allow and surrender to life? Is it living in the present moment that has the entry point to my higher self, or is it power for me to have?

The energy knows when we are present and this is where we are tapped into consciousness, which is where all is held in answers… Right? Deep, I know.

Purpose in Life

I am on an adventure to purpose; the journey that I chose every second in the direction of this highway I am on. The key here is I AM NOT ALONE or POWERLESS. All I gotta do is listen and hear from the powers (God/Spirit/Guides) of the wisdom it holds and carries for me/us. As I start to awaken to this new life my only saving grace to move on is leaning into the compass within, that is directly connected to my God to guide me.

I dread to see this month of December for many reasons. I have to face many celebrations that have profound meaning of BIRTH, the birth of my son Jesse on the 15th and the birth of Jesus on the 25th. For some odd reason, as I write this, I feel a sense of peace within my rolling tears of these two events knowing they are together. I am entering the hardest month, and I pray for strength in going through it with the heavy heart I carry. I am to welcome all of it as it is my unique story of events on this adventure of my purpose here on earth.

Everything I was teaching Jesse is echoing right back to me to learn what I taught. I can hear him saying, "Remember, Mom, you reap what you sow;" thanks, son. This quote has so many magnitudes of ways in perceptions, but all come back to the same message of a boomerang effect. What you give comes back, in so many ways.

If you have faith you have an open mind, and with that you also have infinite possibilities. I am to remember that who I am inside is the speckle of the greatest piece of the ALL, which is why we are all of the ONE.

This human process and understanding of the bigger picture is paramount. It all starts with pieces, and these pieces are all aligned to fit exactly in their place in the puzzle, which is our life. Keep an open vessel, it will happen right in front of your/my eyes.

Private Investigator

I jumped out of bed to write this. Journaling holds a recorded timeframe of pieces of information that will be part of the puzzle of my life. It's a recorded timeframe that later on, in our awakening in awareness, that instills AHA's into perspective. It's a roadmap of questions being answered or a question period. Journaling is a cue and guidance from Spirit, our higher self that is sending us a message. You will only feel the urge to do it and wonder why, but you trust your intuition, so you do it. There is a reason. Journaling is the practiced development of the private investigator of your deepest knowledge. It's an assistant to your inner wisdom, awareness, nonjudgmental discoveries and healings; a place to let go of the past hurts and claim the beauty and freedom of this new higher version of the self. Journaling is a place where the excitement of remembering when and putting the clues together, and the igniting of the euphoria followed by the deep emotions of the event sets in. A welcoming place to have moments unfold right in front of our eyes. Life gives us the answers when we pay attention to all of the steps we take. It's all right in front of us. We are our own private investigators that lead us to the truths and facts.

DECEMBER 3, 2022

Life is Easier Pen to Paper

When I put pen to paper and get out of my own way, I start with these words: Dear God (we need to be heard and God is always listening), when I struggle to do something it's now a sign I'm not trusting the process. I put faith on the back burner and start the negative emotions. So I just stop it all, rearrange my thinking and get realigned with the power that will set me straight and free. I'm writing my way through healing, awakening and manifesting desires, coming from a place of experiencing it already. It takes practice, as the conditioning we have been programmed with is neurologically engrained. Practice gets us off the hollowed beaten path onto a newly surfaced balanced road.

I know my mission and purpose is to get out there and share my story(ies), because it will open the door for so many to step through because they hold the only key that fits. I did not have this Soul experience to just keep it and stay with it alone. It is to be shared to give hope, peace, joy and Love to others. You know you gotta start somewhere, and it is here and now. I have too much to share and quest. To be selfish would be to do nothing, nor would any greatness be birthed. Journaling is my connection to my higher power, and miraculous things happen and unfold all the time.

DECEMBER 6, 2022

Question Period

I'm so feeling this in the pit of my gut of my personal awakening and feeling and knowing of these words, "There's got to be more to this point of living with the loss of my son." I know I am not given this to experience the crushing emotions to be found on the floor after being slammed into a brick wall of grief, and that there be nothing afterwards.

No, there is more, and this is bringing me to wonder and start the question period of it all. It's to start the questions about the why's, what, who, where, and when. I have had an early grief awareness of evolution as Jesse knew from our relationship that I would get the meaning of the signs I receive from him. He knew/ knows who to go through to get a message to me and that I would know it was him. This is beyond and nothing shy of a transcendence of an awakening to be taught to all of us. I pray for daily signs and continued questions, and seek out others in Divine guidance for messages held in that experience. This is where I feel the ecstatic excitement of what is to come, and create an awareness shift from this whole experience of losing a son and the power that grief holds.

Masking Pain

Turning the pain of addiction into saving lives. Yes, through my direct line above and to anyone truly connected. Jesse knows where to go because he knew what suffering in silence felt and meant.

Mastering masking the pain to numb even temporarily; his Soul knew the 5 W's on Earth and the Spirit world.

This is only the beginning and such huge things will be brought down and into the lives that will change because of my Spiritual intuition and connection to Spirit.

New Me

I put my pain upfront to be tasted in every morsel. Why? So I can grow and expand. Every morsel is a piece that holds a story and that story has emotions that hold a truth of awareness.

I got to sit and savour it all without fear, worry or judgment and allow myself to say what comes through.

This is how I grow, evolve, and expand into the NEW ME. I welcome this part and release my original version as I have been REBIRTHED through pain that has given me extra sensors that are deep and new to my being.

I am looking out from a mountain top and see a whole new world with a meaning that I feel deep in my Soul. Every cell is in EMERGENCE of new vitality. I need to take my time as I discover and uncover this whole new me. I take it slow and befriend this new entity I am emerging from. My five senses are tweaked to high vibes, but I know and feel my inner wisdom and connect with it, which in a way brings curiosity and intuition from my Soul and Spirit.

DECEMBER 25 & 26, 2022

Step Closer

The step closer to my vision of the co-creation of my own personal journey journal. This is to help others into the discovery of themselves. How this over time produced a piece by piece (from seeds) subject to the puzzle. The long-awaited creation of my own journal.

Yes, I have been inspired by Michael A. Singer's *The Untethered Soul* (who wouldn't,) and truthfully it all started with an inspiration, a spark that was awaiting the flicker of our own internal flame and fire.

We all have it, we need to feed that spark, ember even, just when we thought there was nothing left.

It's the SOUL that is awaiting for the true SELF to show up, and to dance to the new flames ignited within and to shine like never before. This is the NEW ME, and I'm gonna be as bright and beautiful as a "wish upon a star."

DECEMBER 27, 2022

I Know

The more I go, the more I grow and know what I need to do. I know what matters. I know it's my best life to be lived as authentic and unique as I possibly can. I know I have one life with an unknown end date. I know I have a meaning that matters to me. I know this will be shared with others. I know this life is totally left to me, and how I will be myself.

My saving grace, to step towards living again I had to ask what I already had inside me and have had for most of my life. I had it from a young age, so why complicate life by thinking you have to reinvent yourself? WHEN IT'S ALREADY THERE AND ALWAYS HAS BEEN, IT'S JUST THE FACT OF TAKING TIME TO SIT WITH IT IN SILENCE.

For me, it's the famous meaning of the threes, which are Journaling, Horses and Photography. What beautiful and magical resources they represent. I don't have to search as I already have it and it's a part of me, my Soul. I just have to continuously be with myself, and it is an automatic and authentic operation and co-creation with my God, Spirit, Universe.

It's all the power greater than myself and where my faith and beliefs lie. And trust me there is no room for doubt, as the pieces always show up in fashions that are totally unexpected. All I have to do, at times the hardest, is show up and be present for what is in my immediate moment of presence. A time to show what I am made of, not what happened to me. For me, this is the trilogy of the essence of connection to my Soul self. I just re-read my words, and this is such an awareness of truths for me. The ongoing journey of life with heart no matter what events, experiences, or emotions arise, is a way of finding answers or meaning. Where does this piece of my puzzle fit? What is its content and context in relation to my Soul's evolution?

For me, helping me to live again is doing what I always wanted, to create my own journal.

I have been given so many signs I need to honour the opportunity that is clearly shining its light on the path to be followed through, to bring it to fruition. I will never be at peace if this is not followed through. I will only have regrets and shame, and that is not the deal. I am to do this and share my heart and experiences to help others, and feel the Love Power of deepest trust and connection and joy of knowing Jesse has a huge input in this project. Oh, I feel it, and the inspirational coin that came full circle back to me is definitely to be part of this journeying journal, and it is one heck of a Power Tool.

DECEMBER 28, 2022

Life Is Unpredictable

Four days left until the end of 2022 arrives. Who could have predicted this year of my life? NOBODY… BUT God knows. What did I learn, observe, grow, and admire? Was I better this year than in other years? Surrender comes to mind and allows me to observe people, things and places. Gratitude is a huge one as it embraces surrendering. To allow, mostly builds faith and trust and develops a Power connection of my personal wisdom.

I had no choice in what came my way in August, the most devastating day of my life came: a tragic and traumatic sudden loss of my Jesse. I was "all of a sudden" brought into a whole new world in slow motion, and I went into shock. I continuously look side to side, front and back. I don't see a thing, that's the reflection of my inner world, empty.

How do I even fathom a celebration of the New Year? I don't, that's how. A whole new way of life is going to be birthed for me. I don't know what that will look like for me, but I certainly welcome God and Spirit guides, my Angels and my loved ones who passed to show me my way to my new life, because I have not got a clue nor interest to figure it out. I have enough strength to say I leave it all in their hands because I can't.

JANUARY 1, 2023

I Pray

PRAY to the trilogy, the name of the Father, the Son and the Holy Spirit, all part of the ONE. I take a piece of it and light it up within myself.

I pray for personal miracles and evolutions and transformation in my growth forward.

I pray for bits of fog to lift. There is a piece being uncovered about my healing, and it brings in light.

I pray for this unknown road to be paved with blessed rocks as I step on each one, and sit with each meaning until the next one appears.

I pray for clarity in direction and cleanse my pain with Love.

I pray to deepen my Love and live life as I am guided above greater capacity.

I pray for connection to deepen with the Spirit world and receive the messages for me.

I pray for the greatest co-creativeness I have ever had and build; the unknown service work and creation of doing greatness with people into a known life never imagined.

I pray to co-create Jesse's work on earth to fruition, i.e. my own personal journal I am creating at this moment, and to have a special coin with the meaning that came from Jesse, to share with all and for me to "reach for the Stars."

I pray for it to serve all that needs it.

I pray to somehow work with people suffering from addiction.

I pray to put my own personal Love of Photography to the world with words as quotes to have an impact on my readers.

I pray to bring my horses forward in the healing world like never before, to co-create a change for all who need this transformation into desired tomorrows.

I pray for my personal healing journey.

I pray for continued Angels to show up like they have.

I pray for inspiration, courage and health.

Today holds infinite wisdom and possibilities, what will it be all about?

I am the actor of my life; God is the master scriptwriter, and I remain open to receiving and following according to the necessary actions.

JANUARY 3, 2023

Love Speaks

I take my fears and doubts and transmute them to Love, white light emanating, expanding from my heart into the infinite. When Love speaks through my heart it's super powerful. I claim it for me. I hold the key to the door from my old self to the new.

Emergence of the new me, I say yes to. I step through the fog as it lifts. My Love and light is burning through this fog, and I EMERGE onto the steps and into my power and with God the Universe. I step into it all, fully expanded and I say yes to all that I am; Love, light, abundance, wisdom, aligned with source, clarity. I say yes to all that I am. (Jesse please don't leave me again I beg you. I need to feel our connection more now than ever before. We have work to do as we talked about. I'm showing up in a hot mess and all. I know I have greater things to do and to accomplish.) God show me the way; I am ready. My pain has/is motivating me into a greater meaning of my life and to go forth in the world in ways that I have always carried, within the knowledge that it's showing me how much Love is within its own energy and ready to be birthed into new creations of its meaning. Life does not stop at devastating tragic pain, it's the beginning of the new when ready. I am here to walk it with you. The loss of a loved one means more Love showing up in ways of creation that would never have been without the loss. I know Jesse is helping and guiding me to do the greater things and to spread his Love of life in hope to all.

JANUARY 5, 2023

Life's Whys & Hows

If you are here reading this it's because I AM a perfect fitting piece to your puzzle, your life. The puzzle is a representation of the picture scene of your life. What does this scene look like? How many completed experiences are you seeing? What pieces are left missing from those times and moments? Can you find that one missing piece and put it in its place once and for all?

My biggest piece that is missing in my heart is broken and shattered, and this is where the pieces are lost. Little by little my pieces are found with meaning and placed in their carved-out space waiting to be filled in its newest environment. It's a totally foreign piece like an organ transplant and time will tell how it is accepted and/or rejected. My Soul came to learn and to be free to do so. I don't want to be in its way to stop it; I want to partake in the process and evolution. One way to do this mastery of emotion as a private investigator of our own searches, is by being curious about WHYS AND HOWS. This got me my answers and of course with the connection to my Creator.

JANUARY 12, 2023

Healing & Change

This is where healing and change is taking place. For me, this is exactly what is occurring each day. I've cocooned myself to dive into, allow and surrender to the emotions of grief to flow; crucial to go through this process, the discovery of the self on my new road of life.

I need to re-strengthen, ask questions, and know the answers to the new ground and soil I will be stepping onto when I am ready. This will give me some unknown territory of allowing and welcoming the next following stages of the seasons.

I am doing this once by fully submerging into the waters of grief as I now know there is a meaning of the new me that will EMERGE with the greatness of Love, strength and hope; holding my Jesse in my heart with more Love than pain. I also know this moulding of our souls will create a whole new and beautiful message to others in support service work built around the grieving gift.

JANUARY 13, 2023

The Grace of Self

When we get curious about whys and fully understand ourselves, those words are actually "power of prayer" words. Life is a practice of the soul connection and understanding what it came to experience. Words have such a way of switching our inner guidance of the place we are coming from. Do I come from a place of wanting to be right or a place of "my way?" What if we came from a place of Grace in order to deepen our understanding of ourselves? The inner guidance of emotions will be our truth teller, so listen close. When it's a power struggle, your gut is tight and physically agitated. Take a breath and quietly ask for Grace to enter and to assist you for understanding and asking the whys in questions. This is a choice of empowering and transforming into the better and best version of ourselves in true unity with the Spirit. I am not here to change anyone but myself. This is my life practice and how I can guide others. Remember the mirroring of the self is reflected via horses, as I see and guide others in my practice of healing with horses. This is true for everyday living. I practice my life for me, and that is my transformation and why I journal. This is my record of initiated growth. The proof is in my writing of these words; ownership of what I feel. I feel it in my Soul to find the courage to live this truth of the fact that we are all ONE and one is LOVE. I open up to my highest potential. I keep my potential growing and let everyone see me as an inspiration for the change they want to see in themselves. I am no longer playing invisible nor staying isolated or small. I will only go so far before I need to cross that invisible bridge and step into sharing this great wisdom. I will and am showing up in the uncharted waters knowing it holds unlimited magic.

JOANNE MOÏSE-ROUTHIER

Facing the Outside World

I now know why it hurts so much after attempting to go out into the real world; it is because I am not the same. I get hit with the reality of my son's loss, and he is no longer with me to share it all with. I so miss my son. I went on an outing, and I was stung with the guilt of having laughed and moments of enjoying myself, and eating like there was no bottom (I lost so much weight). I soon found myself in twisted turmoil. I felt I left you, Jesse, at home in our sacred place with your photo on the cabinet with the candles I light daily. Realizing that this belief was not so; no matter where I go you are with me in my heart and will forever be connected like we never thought possible; it fkn hurts, Jesse, it's actually unexplainable. One thing I know, you are here with me and show me and continue to guide me and send me signs of what I need. Why you were called to the greater home I will never know. I can find a place of blame no matter who, what, where and when to put my pain towards, but note that place has had its fill. It won't take the pain away, it's a temporary relief of the pain, that's all. There is damage doing that, as more pain is inflicted on others and that is not the deal, ("True That Dog" - Jesse would say,) and Jesse would never inflict pain on anyone. He carried deep internal pain of his own that was never dealt with and only masked. His Love for life and people was infectious, and I will carry and honour his Love forward. The transition of more Love than pain is a two-step dance, or at times four or 10 steps, it happens in time. What I do during the process of my grief, I will only know when it comes. Also, as I honour my pain and dive into its depths and allow it to be felt and talked through with all emotions present, there is always a message with an answer, awareness or healing; even a closeness to the other side. Never underestimate nor fear this deep dive. It is temporary each time. It will be directed by the inner guidance. Trust in it. This is about a dip in and a dip out of grief. As I write this, my knowledge has deepened about this process of grief and is continuously guided. (God I miss you, Jesse).

Just Start

During my life I have experienced four immediate family losses. I actually question: did my Soul come to experience death and heal from it, heal from the fear and experience; to live fully and share how to live life fully?

In what I'm about to emerge into from my submerged time with my grief and listening to my call to heal, and to hear in depth how life works, the Masterpiece of the collective consciousness, I tap into it and hear it, the weaving of life happens right in front of my eyes, when I live in the present moment. I see how each piece is attached to keep moving forward to the other pieces that delivers the Masterpiece life I am creating.

I finished my four month certification program as a Grief Educator with the world-renowned David Kessler. It's amazing what stops at your door to continue on in your journey for your soul's evolution and the continuance of life and healing.

FEBRUARY 4, 2023

Inside Out

My inside has changed forever, my outside has to catch up with this change. I need to find its balance, my scale is tipped over into grief and pain. I have retreated into solace, the pain has become a safe place for me.

Little by little I start my outer world change to reflect my newly birthed self.

Now, I don't mean to stay in pain, I mean to look at the outside world and activate my changed inner world to start expanding around my grief.

My grief has a bigger meaning about who I am, and the daily output into my container holding the grief is growing as I grow larger to hold pain, but also to honour Jesse in the way that he deserves and what he would want for me.

I also have a huge message to share with the world through my grief. I am the Catalyst for helping the ones who are in need through their grief and pain.

FEBRUARY 12, 2023

Depleted

I just realized I'm in the completely depleted healing stages of the wear and tear of the trauma that has taken place in the last six months; exhausted, burnt out, and very little endurance for activities or company. I just woke up to this awareness and I can see how much it takes out of me, and I now wait for the fact I'm walking into mindful healing of myself and my soul.

If it took me six months to get this awakening to the fact I am at a crossroads, then it's going to take that same amount of time or more in just healthcare to heal my depleted self.

This is why I profess that Journaling is an essential healing tool because in writing I just discovered this aha moment, and it has relieved my worries about my present state of well-being.

I feel this is part of my human review like the Souls review in the Spirit world. It's time to take a look at what transpired and where I'm presently at now, which will plainly direct the path of my future.

This came to me from feeling exhausted again, one step forward and ten back.

I decided to sit at the dawn of day with one candle lit just watching the smoke rise. This was a moment to sit in the quiet place, the void, to just be and allow humbleness and awareness to surface. This is just mind-blowing to how the higher self speaks through our consciousness and how we awake to its messages. My intuition spoke loud and clear. Spirit is truly that powerful, and I am super grateful. If I wouldn't be journaling I wouldn't be processing the entirety of the message I am receiving and its meaning.

Now I know to honour myself as this review has changed my trajectory, and to be very attentive to how much I am doing and can handle, so I don't get tipped and spill all over myself and then have to clean it up.

I want to live fully like I never have known before. In order to do this I better take care of myself now.

Pain and heartache can eat you up so fast that you don't even know how far it has taken you down. I must honour this awareness.

Part 4

Living Again

"Whether it's horses or whatever it is you do, it doesn't become an art until your soul goes into what you do."

— Buck Brannaman

JANUARY 5, 2023

My Best Place

The thing is, I am open to receiving, and I tap into the source of God Angel guiding teachers to a higher realm where the power of Truth resides. I have done this all my life; I am able to completely zone out and into the moment and interconnect with these energies. I "weave" with it! I become one with it, and the outside world does not exist at that present time. Such power and beauty are on a magnitude and explainable.

I do this a lot with my horses; they feel me and the place that is my heart and energy. I completely connect in the present Zone; there is no moment like it. I often stare into thin air when I leave me and enter the moment, and it's in a place of wonder and yonder; the closest I get to God's space. There are no words to explain; it's a feeling that can't be taught but can be learned, exactly the way of being in the presence of horses. This is where the magic happens. I am deep, and there is no place like it. It's the next best peaceful place of being, that I witness, feel and know.

Healing Session

My healing session with my herd of four horses. I was drawn to stand at the rails in pure cool sunlight, to observe them as they interacted. My inner experience surfaced in emotions and I saw a deeper side of life. I was seeing the larger outer aura around Max; my right ear deafened in silent calmness like I never felt before. I temporarily thought something was wrong. I had to slowly turn and look 360 degrees around me in slow motion. It was peace visiting me in a way I never felt. You cannot get this type of "feel good" in a pill bottle or from alcohol. It's pure bliss from Spirit that took place. I had no idea this was going to take place, but I knew to follow my draw of intuition for a reason. This moment gave me permission for my heart to speak its truth of pain and for tears to flow. All the while, Max came to stand in support of me. He transferred the blocked pain energies as I watched the exchange transpire right in front of me, and on me. Max came and muzzled my heart area as my tears flooded my face; he then took steps away to shake it off, yawned, licked and chewed, followed by going to the salt block. The rest of the herd never came to interrupt as their innate senses knew what was transpiring; for my personal healing with Max was not to be interrupted, but supported. The others stood facing in all different directions, which they never usually did. I knew they were holding the sacred space of all directions for my protection, while I was in a vulnerable state in my healing. As time went on and more healing transferred, I can say it was a deep, profound healing that took place. My state of mind and physical heaviness were recalibrated to a level of lightness that I so welcomed and needed, but was unaware of until my head showed up for me when they knew I was ready. This experience can only be told from my inner words, as everyone has their exact profound experience meant only for them. Not one will ever compare to another. All I can say is it is beyond therapeutic, beyond imaginable, unexplainable.

The Void

I follow my gut intuition, knowing it is the key to what needs to show up in my personal evolution as I connect to commune with the Divine. Follow and trust the pieces. They all hold information. Keep in mind that it's all an interconnection. The desire for communion with my horses as messengers happens in a sacred space where there is nothing. The void paradoxically holds everything when you connect to Source. There is nothing like it, nothing. So you see how it takes place; these seeds of information are sewn all the time. It's all there for us if and when we shift to a whole new self and start trusting and connecting to Spirit, and just listen; intuition is never wrong. This is where the magic is unveiled.

JANUARY 19, 2023

Faith & Trust

I just finished a gratitude meditation, and this is what came of it. I intentionally went into the VOID where only God and I are one. I felt the presence, and tears rolled; my heart ached, and I allowed this emotion to rise and to feel. Whatever was to emerge from me did. I fully let my Soul go free and do what it came to do. I watched as I opened up to the infusion of the Holy Spirit within myself, knowing the Divine roadway is in his energy. I ask to receive today's wisdom, healing and messages. I have complete permission to be the recipient of the Great as I know I have only to surrender and allow. I am completely at the mercy of will and grace to come into me, to live for today as I know it is the only way. My faith and trust are building each day as I get off my knees and gain the strength to stand. Stand without the weight of the world on me. I don't have the desire to do so, and that is not my life's direction. The truth is with God, and leaning more and more into him is my non-negotiable way of living now. I pay attention. My arrival to finding God/Divine in these depths is not short of any pain, but also my miracle saving grace with many messengers and Angels showing up.

January 23, 2023

Fearless

Just starting the journey of where I am at this moment. I know I have the content and the context of my messages. I feel I am missing the pieces of trust and faith, but deeper is the WHY. Why am I holding back? What is holding me back? I may not know now, and waste more time to start to even try to figure it out, (it's safe here) instead of grabbing onto the reins and bringing in all I have, like the warrior I am. Start to show up and take my desires seriously, and honour Jesse like I said I would. Do I want to live with the shame of not doing it, and devalue all the showing of signs Jesse sent me? I have more than enough to share, so what is blocking me? FEAR…? No way; I have been through the worst loss a human can go through, so there is no room for fear. I only have momentum to gain moving forward. No matter what my life's lessons and teachings will be, they will all be to help and guide me in my personal evolution to live life fully. I am open armed to receive it all and embrace it all to the max.

Grieving Fully – Living Fully

How can being in the hardest, darkest and most painful times create such a meaningful purpose for me for the rest of my life? I was shown the direction to do it and start my book/journal so strongly. How can I ignore it? I would be doing such a disservice to mySELF by keeping my Soul under lock 'n key; the opposite of what it needs to be in its freedom to be, and what it came here to learn and experience. Who am I to stop such beauty from emerging? Why would I pursue such a damaging and troubling continuance of struggles when life can be so beautiful? My Soul spoke loud and clear, to listen and to create. I will be led all the way as I put my faith and trust in the powers that be, to continue the conversations and interactions with my Soul as I carry it to fruition. Watch the magic unfold. One day, I will hold the creation of "cause and effect" in my hand: my book. I do not and will not dishonour myself nor Jesse and let fear be the driver. I would be haunted for the rest of my days, and I have been shown way too many times to listen and honour my heart's desires. Don't let fear rob the way of proudly standing in the arena. I am doing and creating something for the greater good and service to those who need it. This is my new world; I stand tall in my arena, and those who criticize are the ones standing on the outside with their own fears. I, step by step with all my emotions, entered the arena to create and do what my Soul came to witness and experience. I am the actor in the movie playing, and God is the director.

JANUARY 27, 2023

The Magic

Tears mean I have had a connection with my loved one. I followed my intuition of staying in my pain. It is a connection in grief from our hearts as it opens. I remember saying to a friend that my veil is very thin, so I am really close to the heavens. I may have scared her off by knowing this is possible and that I am there. Anyway, it's all true and real what I feel and am going through. I receive the validation just by following where I am led to go next. It shows me; the magic of trusting the feelings. We have to allow all grief to come up, as that is the channel to connect with our loved ones. Pain and Love are connections to our loved ones. My awareness of my grief process is not just going through it; there are messages. When the messages from our loved ones come through, it changes the meaning of grieving; it's a pure connection through a channel with the Divine.

I am a new being on a new journey with a new purpose, and I hold new meaning. I have new levels of lessons and evolution in my path of life now. I said a new world is out there, no, not exactly; it is me that is NEW, going out in the already existing and moving on of the world. I am not the same; I am brand new. There is such an awareness in how I wrote all along, as I could feel things that were happening and how I was feeling and questioned them. I always saw everything as miracles and magic. I wouldn't change a thing in my grief; so much has come through in the devastation of Jesse's transition to his destination, which we will all someday have to experience. Going into grief deeper and deeper opens up the channel to communicate. This is what I did, not knowing what was happening, and that is why I followed and listened to the signs I received from Jesse communicating with me. I feared getting stuck in life and emotionally challenged if I didn't fully grieve. I can attest with my whole being; there is a meaning with a purpose that miraculously showed up for me.

JANUARY 30, 2023

The Channels

Part of grieving is going through the memories that emerge from pain. It will bring a smile or laughter even in short intermittent moments. This is the spark of Love flickering in our hearts. Do not deny grief to be felt as we do such a disservice to ourselves and our loved ones. One channel of connection resides in grief, and that is where, believe it or not, our hearts are opening up like never before. It thins the veil between us and the other side.

JANUARY 31, 2023

 Where Now

Where do I go from here? I am so wondering this as I enter into my new life and become a version I never knew nor even thought possible. I must start in my new life and serve as I wish to. A bigger meaning awaits me. I meditate to be in touch with my guides to show me. I release all that does not help me and claim my birthright of Love in the name of Grace.

Fear Not

I am a brave Soul to bear down fully in my grief and come up with all of my in touch guided spiritual messages along with Jesse's guidance, my thinned out veil as my heart opens more each time and that I heal in whatever comes to the surface. No one can replicate what I do and produce because no one has my Soul, energy, or vibration behind what I create, and my connection to Source. I clearly state, don't waste time in comparing yourself to anybody and find yourself discouraged or allow fear to seep in. You dishonour yourself. Besides, it never works anyway, and it's a potential rabbit hole to fall into and harder to get out of. So listen to your Soul and don't quit moving with whole heartiness to create organically and uniquely. What will that look like and feel like? Fear not; start it and do it, now.

FEBRUARY 7, 2023

My Soul's Fire

To the best of my ability, I am choosing to live fully. Why? I do have a choice, and I made it from the grace of facing the fact I was heading down the Y roadway to live life, the alternative to die a slow life.

The fire in me is a rebirth from the deepest pain that happened due to the traumatic loss of my son, Jesse. I know the fire in me has started with the flickering embers that remained. The more I walk alongside my horses, the more I know the fire inside is burning with all of my heart. It will come to fruition as that fire holds such a message and a power for the world, and myself. The fire rebirth has totally burnt away the old me; "I will never be the same."

The new me is being birthed as I speak. This I know from the core of my body, Heart and Soul. My horses are actually on fire as well. I have spent the process of healing time with them, and they walk alongside me and hold me through it all, and whatever is to come. My Grief will never die off, but I will evolve and emerge in an unimaginable way, and a new meaning will take place. I will never replace the Love I have for Jesse. It's Jesse's strength and connection that is pulling me through now. My Faith in the unknown will be mind-blowing for what is to come in my world on fire. I Love you all. I couldn't do this without all your Love and support, and kindness. You are truly Angels.

FEBRUARY 15, 2023

Thank God For Horses

A place where I am held, heard and witnessed, where the knowledge of a shift takes place; an honourable, sacred and safe place to let down my guard. Where the energies of the land support me, and its power carries me fully. Magnetism is where change takes place within my heart. There is an energized vibration that holds the identity of who I truly am, a freedom feeling unknown to my transformation in my Grief, into the Love of Jesse. There is so much power in grief; it contains the rebirth of the new me. Here I feel the change holding me step by step without shame, guilt, or judgement. I can let the tears flow, and I can then witness my rebirth happening with each step. Being present with the Horses, I know they truly are the miracle messengers of healing in my purely cognitive and spiritual awareness. I allow the healing to take place as the grief surfaces, and ready to be released layer by layer. I trust in this process of healing like unknown modalities that don't exist, but this one does. Thank God for horses. I feel this is a sacred space for the grieving Souls that find themselves lost and confused and need fine-tuning of their personal guidance with Love and Compassion within their forward momentum. The transformation is nothing shy of miraculous and amazing; this I know to be true from the depth of my own grief healing, this I know.

The Flame Of Love

The flame represents great meaning. It burns if you touch it. It burns in pain afterwards because you Love that flame, that for me is Jesse. He was a walking piece of truth everywhere he went. He had so much Love to give and was genuinely charismatic to the end. Sure, he had faults too, like all of us. His Love for people and life was infectious. I was gifted with the flame of Love: my son. His flame is carried in my heart, and it's beginning to burn bigger and brighter as I transition from pain, where I couldn't see any light at all of the flickering flame in the distance. It's trying to ignite, on and off again and then just smouldering smoke at times, to smoke where I couldn't breathe; finding out in order to see and feel the flame that holds the Love. The brightness and force of a flame is what you feed it. Will it be a roaring fire with beautiful flames? Or will it be just embers and smoke?

This process will fluctuate, but it will get to where it feels comfy and cozy to sit with it more and more.

FEBRUARY 17, 2023

The Great Awakening – Horses

Horses are spirit animals. Horses are the closest to God. Horses are messengers of God in connecting to our truth and our personal Spiritual Awakening and growth in our journey. Yes, I know, as I have witnessed the unbelievable to believable. Horses automatically awaken us; they heal us layer by layer through the pain just by being in their presence. The horses are the awakeners to our Souls. Horses wake us up to Who We Are inside and our connection to Spirit and the power that we hold within. Horses are the closest thing to getting an Awakening to your true self.

I just put all the pieces together. I found where horses belong in our universe as messengers from God, to uncover the great mystical transmissions they hold for us.

I know I have a connection to Spirit, but now I have direct messengers holding information I receive through my intuition. Horses heal and bring, right under our noses, what we have unconsciously known, making it conscious just by being with them. We get nonverbal communication that is an automatic conveyance of Heart to Heart coherence and limbic brain transference; it's science in the present moment at work. Breath brings us to the present moment in front of us; it's a regulation of its own when we find ourselves in emotional trouble. You end up in a greater space of mind from the automatic connection that happens. This is the great secret of horses and Spirit/God. It is beyond powerful as I embody this new awakening surging throughout my body. I am still shaking from this awakening to the Spirit of this magical fine-tuning of me. This is why I connect to horses the way I do in the most profound depths unknown to many. Horses are key openers to our Souls and the deep connectors to the DIVINE.

FEBRUARY 19, 2023

Letting Go

I let go of fear, limitations, and blocks that hold me back. Stop wasting time trying to figure out what those are. I acknowledge them and move through them with all that I have and just go for the vision of creation I hold within.

I claim the Divine power within me and demand to co-create with the Divine as I move forward.

Life is what I make it, and I know it's all within me. It is there, and it's called the inner wisdom, where my higher Self resides, and that is my direct line to Spirit that I hold in my Soul.

WHY would I not tap into this power and let the rest that is holding me hostage to stay stagnant from Fear? Fear of what? Past programming?

I am moving on from surviving to creating. I was born to create, so why not honour myself and create? This is the most rewarding way to grow on this adventurous journey. This is where and how my Soul experiences itself with my full permission and surrender, what it came to experience.

I get out of the way and fully Embrace Life because it is beautiful. The unlimited magic.

FEBRUARY 20, 2023

Daily Prayer

Divine Mary

Full of Grace

Holy Mother of all creations

Fill my mind with your thoughts

Open my Heart with your Love

Ignite within my Spirit the Eternal Flame of Grace.

As I walk your Path

Of Love and Grace

Unlimited Miracles Manifest through me.

-Sherrie Dillard

The following words, "WHO AM I and WHERE AM I GOING," brought up tears and emotions of fear and wonder. These words must be sat with to ponder the answers, as I sit and meditate with Mother Mary to help me and guide me. I also invite my Angels to surround me in support of their whispers, ready for me to hear.

I sit and ask Who I Am? What is my WHY in life? What is my passion and my purpose?

My pain of losing Jesse when reality hits, over and over, the pain begins the cycle in disbelief; I pray for help in my Soul's evolution on my journey along the way, and grow my connection to Jesse from the other side.

FEBRUARY 23, 2023
FINAL JOURNAL ENTRY

The Wake-Up

Things may come in a way you never thought of; a way that is effortless to manoeuvre, or it may be difficult, even detrimental (I'm crying now). But I know this one thing that built me up prior to the loss of my son Jesse, was my learning and teachings that showed up in my way of life, is my Spirituality. It's the learning to find the end results of my visions in life that were difficult pieces, but I didn't know the tools to use. The tools that I learned along the way have filled my toolbox, but are so light to carry. The opposite actually, the more you put in, the lighter it gets, not the heavier. The more I learn in my life, and it is a lot (I'm a seeker and a leader), the stronger I become in handling difficult times. More and more things arise that are effortless to me. My spirituality and commitment to building up my connection to Spirit has been key for me. I studied and sought mentors to help me along my path of all the questions and the Whys, to understand the teachings and lessons I have experienced. During this journey, it made me face vulnerability and humbleness, both sides of the coin. I WOKE UP!

Learning is uncomfortable, but the end result of working through it is very rewarding and where growth and evolution take place.

I share this to show that all of my learning of desires and life's experiences along the journey of my spiritual path have definitely given me the strength to go through the grief and mourning of Jesse.

Therefore, nobody can tell me where I am at in my present life within my "timely grief," nor deny me anything to do with what I am, feel, or am ready to do. Nobody knows how to dictate where I am at present. So thank you to the ones who have closed doors on me that I tried to open so that I would be aware of this. If I feel ready to start navigating my new world, it is not up to anybody to deny me access. That is for my personal discovery only.

Trust me, while in the deep throes of grief you do not want anything to do with the outside world. My safety zone is my home. Isolation actually describes how it feels. No one could understand my pain, and I didn't want to even hear anyone's thoughts on my "hell life" at the time.

My tears have stopped for the moment, and you know what; there is only one ruler of my life, and that is my GOD.

If I am ready to do the two-step with life, sometimes the ten-step, because I feel ready. I will go at the pace that I'm ready and be carried through its momentum. I trust it. So I dance with life. How are you dancing with life? Are you doing the two or 10-step? What have you learned about yourself lately, or when was the last time you did a self check-in? Get indulged within yourself and write the answers.

I journal every day and this is my one for sure, knowing how to get to the bottom of clarity about my truth of where I am at. I have the proof in my "inner state highway" as I read back in my writings.

"When things are easy, you ride the wave; when things are hard, you are the wave."

I am here today to co-create a legend in my world, to make an impact in shifting change for each and every Soul to get to know themselves. This is my mission and purpose in this lifetime to create a change for the better, especially for the grievers to make it through to the other side. To find self-inspiration and motivation, and the empowerment found from listening to their inner wisdom. We cannot do this alone, and I do not profess to; you do have help by your side, so please reach out.

In Closing

"Let the Flame of my Love Live on in your Heart Forever

- Love Jesse"

My SOUL is forever in EVOLUTION stages of the LEADING guide of my life, moving me FORWARD into welcoming infinite unknown possibilities. (S.E.L.F.)

My one life on Earth, as the Soul I am, is to live and be lived to its maximum with full intention of the emergence of the Soul self. Follow along for the continuing evolution and transformation of loving life to its fullest; embracing the process of experiences no matter what that may look like, as there are always pieces of transformation and evolution of incoming whispers awaiting with the continuous practice of journaling.

Respecting Grief

I respect grief because it holds a golden nugget of wisdom and awareness in the deep throws of its pain. Grief has taught me so much about myself inside, and my outer world's reflections back to me. Sitting with grief shows me I have deep Love and care, and sometimes, unaddressed old wounds. I thank my grief for its teachings on my journey in my personal development, awakening and growth of myself. Grief has taught me how I have grown into and been re-birthed into a new ME, and that there is no way I'd ever want to go back to the previous me. Grief is delicate and to be respected, as it is the carrier of messages awaiting me when I'm ready to receive them. When grieving calls me I attend with an open heart, as it is now a greater piece of me that I have learned to cherish and treasure. Grief's container holds wisdom only I can unfold and decipher. My grief and I have developed a special relationship that will only be understood privately and personally.

I no longer fear grief; I respect it greatly. I listen full-heartedly to my personal "Heart Whispers" in my journey of life.

Joanne

About the Author

In the wake of a devastating loss of her son Jesse, a remarkable spiritual thought leader emerges ready to profoundly impact the world. Meet the compassionate soul behind Horses Healing Hearts, a herd of four majestic beings dedicated to specializing in grief healing.

But why grief, you may wonder? It was a question that echoed in the heart of Joanne Moïse-Routhier, a courageous mother who tragically lost her beloved son, Jesse, in August 2022. Through the depths of despair, she discovered a profound connection to Spirit and Mother Earth, a transformative journey that unveiled an epiphany from the heavens above.

Joanne Moïse-Routhier

With a passion for photography, Joanne captures the exquisite beauty granted upon us by the Creator. From a tender age, she possessed an innate attunement to the world's energies, sensing things beyond her understanding. This led her down a path of curiosity, forging an unbreakable bond with the magic and power woven into every being.

Years of experiences, education, and knowledge beyond the realm of the five senses have bestowed upon her a pearl of wisdom and heightened perception she never dreamt possible. Certified by the esteemed Grief Specialist, David Kessler, and her expertise in Equine Assisted Learning (EAL Canada) has empowered countless clients, proving that hope is attainable, and change is the key to transforming their lives.

In addition to her mastery in grief healing, she holds certifications as an Energy Healer, Reiki Practitioner, SMART Recovery Facilitator and is now a professional speaker. As a frequent guest on the acclaimed *Robust Lifestyles* Podcast (*Divas That Care Network*), she has touched the lives of many. Now, she embraces a new role as a budding author, poised to deliver profound insights to those navigating the treacherous terrain of grief.

To embark on such a journey requires immense courage, resilience, faith and trust in God, and a fire within that transcends the pain of grief. This book is a testament to the indomitable human spirit, a beacon of hope and transformation. Within its pages, the reader will discover the "Golden Nugget"—a profound purpose and meaning that resides deep within our hearts. As grief and Love intertwine a powerful change awaits, one that honours the cherished memories of our loved ones and illuminates a path to healing.

As you delve into this poignant and life-altering book, prepare to be inspired, moved, and forever changed.

www.joannerouthier.com

FB & IG

doublebeauty@outlook.com

Acknowledgments

I couldn't have done it without Carolyn Flower of Oxygen Publishing Agency and her team. Thank you for feeling and capturing what I was inspired to share with the world in helping grieving hearts.

Capturing the grace of this sensitive topic, each and every one had a personal impact during this creation. It was beyond imaginable, and it reached my heart and captured the essence of the words of my memoir.

I thank my daughter, Chantale, and grandson, Ethan, for being there each and every day, holding each other up in Love, kindness and support.

To everyone who showed up in visits, phone calls, text messages, gifts and cards, I call you all my Guardian Angels. Also, the greatest carriers and messengers in guiding me one step at a time, my horses and Jesus.

And finally, to all of you who are here reading this, to be part of your world in your transformation journey.

I Love you all from the deepest piece of my Heart.

A message from Jesse through another...

Hello. I know you probably don't remember me. But I lived next to you on the lower eighth concession when Jesse was in high school and you moved into the blue house in 2000. I know this might seem out of the blue as we weren't very close. But Jesse was a dear friend to me when I needed someone to talk to. I appreciated the man you raised.

I know this might sound a bit weird but I'm a psychic medium and I have a lot of spirits pass through me in my dreams. I had Jesse come to me in my dream last night. He was doing well and smiling so grand. We haven't talked in years but when I woke up to Facebook him, I found out he had passed. So I wanted to take that as a sign to pass on to you that he's doing all right up above. It's not often I have a spirit who has passed, come to me. But I think he wanted to send you a huge hug, as that's what I woke up to this morning. The caress of his arms felt surreal. So here I am passing you on that caress.

Bailey Masson